# COLE B. BRODOSKI

# lost hiker

*guide to surviving the night and getting found*

# Contents

# 1

# introduction

**C**hapter 1: The Importance of Preparedness
In the expansive wilderness, where the unexpected can swiftly transform a simple hike into a fight for survival, being prepared is the linchpin for overcoming the unknown. This opening chapter of "The Lost Hiker Guide: Survive the Night and Get Found" emphasizes the pivotal role of readiness before setting foot on any outdoor journey.

**A. Understanding the Wilderness** Before immersing ourselves in the details of survival, it's crucial to recognize the wilderness for what it truly is – a realm of both enchantment and hazard. The magnetic pull of unexplored trails and the marvels of nature often divert attention from the potential risks lying beneath the surface. From abrupt weather shifts to unexpected wildlife encounters, the wilderness commands respect and necessitates a proactive approach.

**B. The Cascading Impact of Preparedness** Preparedness transcends a mere checklist of items; it embodies a mindset that can mean the difference between life and death. While being prepared doesn't shield one from challenges, it significantly augments the ability to face and navigate the unknown. The cascading impact of preparedness extends not only to the individual but also to the broader community and the search and rescue teams ready to respond.

**C. Overview of the Guide** Tailored for hikers facing the unexpected, this guide aims to furnish you with the knowledge and skills essential to confront the wilderness. Unfurling as a comprehensive manual, it delves into pre-trip preparations, navigation tactics, shelter construction, water and food acquisition, signaling for rescue, and mental fortitude. Each chapter is crafted to empower you with practical strategies, transforming panic into confidence in the face of adversity.

**D. Empowering Lost Hikers** By grasping the significance of preparedness, readers are urged to approach their wilderness excursions with a proactive mindset. "The Lost Hiker Guide" is not merely a survival tool; it stands as a companion, offering a wealth of knowledge derived from experience and expertise. Its objective is to cultivate a community of well-informed and capable hikers who not only cherish nature's beauty but also respect its potential challenges.

As we embark on this expedition through the pages of "The Lost Hiker Guide," let the importance of preparedness resonate within you. The wilderness, with all its uncertainties, becomes a canvas where your readiness paints a picture of survival, resilience, and the triumphant spirit of those who navigate the unknown.

2

# Pre-Trip Preparations

**C**hapter 2:

Before venturing into the wilderness, ensuring you're adequately prepared is paramount for a safe and enjoyable journey. This chapter outlines in detail the essential pre-trip preparations, focusing on sharing your itinerary and packing key items for navigation, shelter, water, food, first aid, and communication.

**A. Share Your Itinerary**

1. **Detailed Planning**: Plan your route meticulously, including start and end points, potential rest stops, and estimated timeframes for each leg of your journey.

2. **Emergency Contacts**: Share your itinerary with a trusted friend, family member, or local ranger station. Include details such as your expected return time and contact information for all members in your party.

3. **Check-In Procedure**: Establish a check-in protocol with your designated contacts, specifying how often you'll communicate and what to do if they don't hear from you.

## B. Pack Essentials

1. **Navigation Tools** a. **Map and Compass**: Carry a detailed topographic map of the area along with a reliable compass. Familiarize yourself with basic navigation skills, such as reading contour lines and using declination. b. **GPS Device**: Consider a **GPS** device with pre-loaded maps and extra batteries. While technology can be a valuable tool, always have a traditional map and compass as a backup.

2. **Shelter** a. **Weather-Appropriate Shelter**: Choose a shelter suitable for the expected weather conditions. Options include a lightweight tent, a durable tarp, or an emergency bivvy. b. **Insulation**: Pack a sleeping bag and insulating pad to stay warm during chilly nights. Even in warmer climates, nighttime temperatures can drop significantly.

3. **Water and Purification Methods** a. **Hydration System**: Carry a durable water bottle or hydration bladder with a minimum capacity of two liters. Ensure it's easily accessible during your hike. b. **Water Purification**: Pack water purification tablets, a portable water filter, or a UV purifier. Familiarize yourself with the water sources along your route and plan to refill when available.

4. **Food** a. **Caloric Dense Foods**: Choose lightweight, high-energy foods like energy bars, trail mix, and dehydrated meals. Consider your dietary preferences and any potential allergies. b. **Emergency Rations**: Include a small stash of non-perishable emergency rations, such as energy gels or compact meal replacement bars.

5. **First Aid Kit** a. **Personalized Kit**: Customize your first aid kit to address specific medical needs and potential risks on your journey. Include items such as adhesive bandages, antiseptic wipes, pain relievers, blister pads, and any necessary prescription medications. b. **First Aid Training**: Equip yourself with basic

first aid knowledge. Consider taking a wilderness first aid course to enhance your skills in handling injuries or medical emergencies.

6. **Communication Devices** a. **Cell Phone**: Bring a fully charged cell phone with important emergency contacts saved. Keep it in a waterproof case to protect it from the elements. b. **Two-Way Radio**: Consider a two-way radio for communication in areas with limited or no cell reception. Ensure you and your hiking partners are on the same frequency. c. **Personal Locator Beacon (PLB)**: In remote areas, carry a **PLB** that can send distress signals and your location to emergency services.

By diligently preparing and packing these essentials, you lay the foundation for a safer and more enjoyable wilderness experience. Each item serves a specific purpose, contributing to your overall preparedness and ensuring you're equipped to handle whatever challenges the wilderness may present.

# 3

# Staying Calm and Assessing the Situation

**C**hapter 3:
When faced with the unexpected in the wilderness, maintaining a clear and level-headed approach is crucial. This chapter delves into the art of staying calm and systematically assessing the situation, offering detailed instructions, methods, techniques, and examples for each step.

**A. Stop and Stay Put**

1. **Immediate Halt**: The moment you realize you may be lost or facing an unforeseen challenge, stop walking. Continuing aimlessly can lead you further away from known landmarks.

2. **Mark Your Location**: If possible, leave a visible marker at your current location. This could be as simple as tying a bright piece of clothing to a tree branch. This not only helps rescuers but can also serve as a reference point if you need to backtrack.

3. **Stay Calm and Collected**: Take a few deep breaths to calm your nerves. Panic can cloud judgment, making it harder to think rationally. Remind yourself that staying put is a strategic decision.

## B. Evaluate Surroundings

1. **360-Degree Observation**: Slowly turn in a full circle, carefully observing your surroundings. Look for distinctive features, landmarks, or any familiar elements from your pre-trip research.
2. **Identify Water Sources**: Locate nearby water sources, as they are critical for survival. The sound of running water might indicate a stream, and dense vegetation could be a sign of moisture-rich areas.
3. **Terrain Assessment**: Note the type of terrain you are in – whether it's mountainous, wooded, or a combination. This information can help you orient yourself based on your pre-trip knowledge.

## C. Take Stock of Resources

1. **Inventory Check**: Assess the items in your backpack. Ensure you have all the essentials, including navigation tools, shelter, water, and food. Identify any tools or equipment that can aid in signaling or navigation.
2. **Prioritize Resources**: Determine the quantity and condition of your resources. Conserve water and food, especially if it might take some time before rescue arrives. Prioritize your needs based on the duration you anticipate being in the wilderness.
3. **Emergency Supplies**: If your situation requires an overnight stay, access your shelter and insulation. Make a plan for creating a safe and comfortable sleeping environment.

## D. Mental Preparedness

1. **Positive Self-Talk**: Engage in positive self-talk to maintain a

resilient mindset. Remind yourself of your preparedness and capabilities. Focus on the steps you can take to improve your situation.

2. **Set Realistic Goals**: Establish achievable short-term goals, such as finding a recognizable landmark or water source. Breaking down the challenge into smaller tasks can make the situation more manageable.

3. **Mindfulness Techniques**: Practice mindfulness techniques to stay grounded. Techniques such as focusing on your breathing or finding a point of stillness in your surroundings can help alleviate anxiety.

**Example Scenario:** Imagine you've been hiking in a dense forest, and the trail suddenly disappears. You stop, tie a brightly colored bandana to a nearby tree, and take a moment to breathe. Turning around, you notice a distinctive rock formation that you remember passing earlier. Evaluating your resources, you find a small stream nearby and decide to follow it, knowing that water sources often lead to larger trails. As you move forward, you mentally prepare yourself for the possibility of an overnight stay, ensuring you have your shelter and insulation readily available.

By following these detailed steps and examples, hikers can effectively stay calm, assess their surroundings, take stock of resources, and maintain mental preparedness when faced with unexpected challenges in the wilderness.

4

# Navigation Techniques

**C**hapter 4:

In the wilderness, the ability to navigate effectively is paramount for a lost hiker. This chapter will provide comprehensive instructions, methods, techniques, and examples for utilizing various navigation tools, ensuring you can confidently find your way back to safety.

**A. Map Reading**

1. **Orientation**: Begin by orienting your map to match the landscape. Use prominent landmarks or terrain features to align the map. This step is crucial for understanding your current position and the direction you need to go.

2. **Trail Identification**: Identify the trail or path you were originally following on the map. Note distinctive features such as junctions, elevations, and water bodies to confirm your location.

3. **Comprehending Contour Lines**: Understand contour lines to gauge the terrain's steepness and layout. Closer contour lines indicate steeper terrain, while spaced-out lines suggest a gentler slope.

4. **Updating Your Position**: Continuously update your position on the map as you progress. Mark notable features you encounter to maintain an accurate representation of your route.

**Example Scenario:** Picture yourself on a mountain trail, and you've lost sight of the marked path. You stop, pull out your map, and orient it to the terrain. Identifying a distinct peak to your west, you realize your current location is east of the trail. By referencing the map, you determine the best route to reconnect with the path.

### B. Use of a Compass

1. **Setting Declination**: Adjust your compass to the correct declination for the region. This ensures that your magnetic and true north align, providing accurate directions.
2. **Orienting the Compass**: Hold the compass flat in your hand and rotate your body until the needle aligns with the orienting arrow. The direction of travel arrow now points in the direction you need to go.
3. **Taking Bearings**: Identify a prominent landmark along your desired route, and use the compass to measure the bearing. Follow this bearing to stay on course.
4. **Back Bearing**: If you need to backtrack, use the opposite direction on the compass to take a back bearing. This helps you retrace your steps accurately.

**Example Scenario:** Imagine you've reached a fork in the trail, and uncertainty sets in. By taking a bearing with your compass toward a distinct mountain in the distance, you establish the correct path. As you walk, periodically rechecking your compass ensures you remain on course.

### C. Identifying Landmarks

1. **Prominent Features**: Look for distinctive and easily recognizable features, such as unique rock formations, tree configurations, or mountain peaks.  These landmarks serve as reliable reference points.
2. **Creating Mental Images**: As you hike, create mental images of key landmarks in relation to your route. This mental map aids in retracing your steps if needed.
3. **Recording Landmarks**: Jot down or take pictures of significant landmarks as you progress. This documentation can be invaluable for backtracking or providing reference points for search and rescue teams.

**Example Scenario:** While navigating through a dense forest, you notice a large, twisted tree with a unique shape. You make a mental note of this distinctive landmark and continue on your route. Later, if you encounter uncertainty, spotting the twisted tree assures you that you're on the right path.

### D. Sun and Stars for Direction

1. **Sun as a Compass**: In the Northern Hemisphere, the sun generally rises in the east and sets in the west.  Use this knowledge to determine your direction during daylight hours. In the Southern Hemisphere, the sun's path is reversed.
2. **Star Navigation**: In the absence of city lights, stars can be reliable nighttime guides. The North Star (Polaris) is particularly useful, as it remains relatively fixed in the northern sky.
3. **Shadow Tip Method**: Use the shadow tip method by placing a stick upright in the ground and marking the tip of its shadow. After some time, mark the shadow tip again. The line between the two points represents an east-west direction, with the first mark indicating west.

**Example Scenario:** Picture yourself caught in the wilderness as dusk approaches. By observing the sun's position in the sky and the direction of shadows, you deduce the general east-west orientation. As night falls, the North Star becomes visible, guiding you with its steady presence.

By mastering these navigation techniques, lost hikers can confidently find their way back to safety, relying on maps, compasses, landmarks, and celestial cues. These skills are fundamental for overcoming disorientation and navigating the unknown in the wilderness.

# 5

# Building Shelter

Chapter 5:

When lost in the wilderness, the ability to construct a suitable shelter is crucial for survival. This chapter provides detailed instructions, methods, techniques, and examples for choosing a safe location and exploring various emergency shelter options, including tarp shelters, improvised debris shelters, and clothing insulation.

**A. Choosing a Safe Location**

1. **Consider Terrain**: Look for flat ground away from potential hazards such as cliffs, unstable rocks, or dead trees. Avoid low-lying areas prone to flooding.

2. **Proximity to Resources**: Choose a location near essential resources like water and materials for shelter construction. However, maintain a safe distance from water sources to avoid flooding during rain.

3. **Wind Direction**: Take note of the prevailing wind direction. Position your shelter so that the entrance is facing away from the wind to minimize exposure.

4. **Visibility**: If possible, select a location visible from a distance. This increases the likelihood of being spotted by search and rescue teams.

**Example Scenario:** Imagine finding yourself lost in a dense forest as night falls. After careful consideration, you identify a clearing with a flat surface, away from potential hazards. The clearing is close to a small stream, providing a water source, and it's strategically positioned with the entrance of your shelter facing away from the prevailing wind.

**B. Emergency Shelter Options**

1. **Tarp Shelters**
2. a. **Materials Needed**: Carry a lightweight and durable tarp, cordage (paracord or sturdy twine), and trekking poles or nearby trees.
3. b. **Setting Up a Lean-To Shelter**: i. Tie one end of the cordage to a tree or trekking pole. ii. Extend the tarp over the cordage, creating a sloped roof. iii. Secure the other end of the tarp to the ground, ensuring a taut structure. iv. Use additional cordage and stakes to anchor the sides for stability.
4. c. **Benefits**: Tarp shelters are quick to set up, providing protection from rain and wind. They are versatile and lightweight, making them ideal for emergency situations.
5. **Improvised Debris Shelters**
6. a. **Materials Needed**: Gather sticks, branches, leaves, and any available natural materials.
7. b. **Building a Debris Hut**: i. Create a framework by leaning large sticks against a sturdy base. ii. Cover the frame with smaller branches, leaves, and other debris for insulation. iii. Leave an opening at one end for entry and exit. iv. Create a raised bed inside using leaves or dry grass for insulation from the cold ground.

8. c. **Benefits**: Debris shelters offer effective insulation and protection against the elements. They utilize natural materials and can provide more comprehensive coverage than tarp shelters.
9. **Clothing Insulation**
10. a. **Layering Principle**: Utilize the clothing you have by applying the layering principle. Wear multiple layers to trap warm air close to your body.
11. b. **Improvised Insulation**: If lacking proper clothing, use natural materials such as leaves, grass, or moss to create insulating layers. Stuff clothing with these materials to enhance warmth.
12. c. **Improvised Sleeping Bag**: If stranded without a sleeping bag, wrap yourself in multiple layers of clothing, securing them with belts or cordage to retain body heat.
13. d. **Benefits**: Clothing insulation is readily available and can provide immediate warmth. Layering allows for adjusting insulation levels based on temperature changes.

**Example Scenario:** As night approaches and temperatures drop, you decide to construct an improvised debris hut using fallen branches and leaves. The shelter provides a secure and insulated space, protecting you from the chilling night air and potential precipitation.

By mastering the art of choosing a safe location and constructing emergency shelters such as tarp shelters, improvised debris shelters, and utilizing clothing insulation, lost hikers can significantly improve their chances of surviving the night in the wilderness. These techniques, born out of resourcefulness and adaptability, form the backbone of effective wilderness survival.

# 6

# Securing Water

**C**hapter 6:

Water is a fundamental resource for survival in the wilderness, and knowing how to secure and purify it is paramount. This chapter provides detailed instructions, methods, techniques, and examples for locating water sources and employing various purification methods, including boiling, filtration, and chemical purification.

**A. Locating Water Sources**

1. **Observation and Listening**: Pay attention to the environment for signs of water, such as the presence of vegetation, animal tracks, or the sound of running water. Listen carefully, as the sound of a stream or river can guide you to water sources.
2. **Topographical Features**: Use your map and knowledge of the terrain to identify potential water sources. Valleys, depressions, and low areas are likely locations for streams or ponds.
3. **Animal Behavior**: Observe the behavior of wildlife, as animals often gather around water sources. Birds flying in a specific direction may lead you to water.

4. **Look for Greenery**: Vegetation, especially lush and green areas, can indicate the presence of water. Follow these signs to find water, particularly in arid regions.

**Example Scenario:** Lost in a dry and arid landscape, you notice a cluster of green vegetation in the distance. Recognizing this as a potential indicator of water, you follow the vegetation, eventually discovering a small oasis with a hidden spring.

**B. Purification Methods**

1. **Boiling**
2. a. **Collect Water**: Use a clean container to collect water from the source. If necessary, pre-filter it through a cloth or fine mesh to remove debris.
3. b. **Boil Water**: Place the container over a heat source and bring the water to a rolling boil. Maintain the boil for at least one minute (longer at higher altitudes) to ensure the destruction of harmful microorganisms.
4. c. **Cool Before Consuming**: Allow the water to cool before drinking. Boiling not only kills bacteria and parasites but also eliminates many viruses.
5. d. **Benefits**: Boiling is a simple and effective method, requiring minimal equipment. It is particularly useful when dealing with water contaminated by biological contaminants.
6. **Filtration**
7. a. **Select a Filtration Device**: Choose a portable water filter suitable for wilderness use. Look for filters that can effectively remove bacteria, protozoa, and some viruses.
8. b. **Pre-Filtering**: If the water source is turbid or contains visible debris, pre-filter it using a cloth or fine mesh before passing it through the filter. This helps extend the life of the filter.

9. c. **Follow Manufacturer Guidelines**: Adhere to the instructions provided by the filter manufacturer. Most filters require pumping or squeezing to force water through the filtration system.

10. d. **Benefits**: Filtration is efficient and convenient, providing a quick solution for removing a wide range of contaminants. It's especially useful when dealing with clear water sources.

11. **Chemical Purification**

12. a. **Select Chemical Treatment**: Carry water purification tablets or liquid drops containing chlorine dioxide or iodine. These chemicals effectively kill bacteria, viruses, and some parasites.

13. b. **Follow Dosage Instructions**: Adhere to the recommended dosage provided by the product instructions. Ensure that the chemical treatment is evenly distributed throughout the water.

14. c. **Wait for Activation**: Allow sufficient time for the chemical treatment to take effect. This typically ranges from 30 minutes to four hours, depending on the product and water temperature.

15. d. **Benefits**: Chemical purification is lightweight, compact, and easy to carry. It is an excellent backup method when boiling or filtration is not feasible.

**Example Scenario:** In a situation where your water filter malfunctions, you resort to chemical purification. Following the instructions on the iodine tablets, you treat the collected water, patiently waiting for the recommended activation time before safely consuming it.

By mastering the art of locating water sources and employing purification methods such as boiling, filtration, and chemical purification, lost hikers can ensure a safe and reliable water supply, mitigating the risks associated with waterborne contaminants in the wilderness. These techniques are indispensable for maintaining hydration and overall well-being during a survival scenario.

# 7

# Obtaining Food

**C**hapter 7:
When stranded in the wilderness, sourcing food becomes a critical aspect of survival. This chapter provides comprehensive instructions, methods, techniques, and examples for obtaining sustenance through edible plants, basic foraging tips, fishing and trapping, and preserving energy.

**A. Edible Plants**

1. **Identification Skills**: Acquire knowledge of local flora and be able to identify edible plants. Familiarize yourself with characteristics such as leaf shape, color, and growth pattern. Carry a reliable field guide for reference.

2. **Universal Edible Plants**: Learn about universally edible plants, such as dandelions, cattails, and stinging nettles. These plants are often found in various regions and can provide valuable nutrients.

3. **Test Edibility**: Before consuming any plant, perform the universal edibility test. Start by placing a small part of the plant on your inner wrist or lip and wait for at least 15 minutes. If there is no irritation or adverse reaction, proceed to the next step.

4. **Parts to Consume**: Focus on edible parts such as leaves, stems, and roots. Avoid plants with milky sap or a bitter taste, as these can be indicators of toxicity.

**Example Scenario:** Lost in a forest, you come across a patch of cattails near a water source. Recognizing them as a versatile edible plant, you harvest the young shoots and roots. After testing for edibility, you incorporate them into your makeshift meal.

### B. Basic Foraging Tips

1. **Seasonal Awareness**: Understand the seasonal availability of different foods. Certain plants, fruits, and nuts are more abundant during specific times of the year.
2. **Animal Sign Tracking**: Observe tracks, scat, and other signs of wildlife. Following these indicators can lead you to areas with higher chances of finding edible plants or potential hunting opportunities.
3. **Diversity in Diet**: Aim for a diverse diet to ensure a balance of nutrients. Incorporate a variety of plants, berries, and small animals to meet your nutritional needs.
4. **Ethical Foraging**: Practice ethical foraging by taking only what you need and avoiding the overharvesting of plants. Respect the natural environment and wildlife habitats.

**Example Scenario:** As you forage for food, you notice deer tracks leading to a clearing. Following these tracks, you discover a patch of wild strawberries. Respecting ethical foraging principles, you gather a small quantity, leaving the majority for local wildlife.

### C. Fishing and Trapping Basics

1. **Improvised Fishing Gear**: Craft simple fishing gear using

available materials. Use paracord or twisted vines as fishing lines and fashion hooks from durable plant stems or improvised materials like safety pins.

2. **Selecting Fishing Locations**: Choose spots with potential fish habitats, such as deep pools, undercuts in riverbanks, or areas with submerged rocks. Be patient and observant, watching for ripples or movement in the water.

3. **Improvised Traps**: Construct basic traps using materials in the environment. Simple deadfall traps, snare loops, or funnel traps can be effective for catching small game.

4. **Understanding Animal Behavior**: Familiarize yourself with the habits and behavior of local wildlife. This knowledge enhances your ability to set traps or position yourself strategically for fishing.

**Example Scenario:** By a riverbank, you fashion a makeshift fishing rod using a flexible branch and a section of paracord. Patiently casting your line into a promising pool, you eventually catch a small fish. Nearby, you set up a deadfall trap using rocks, hoping to secure additional sustenance.

### D. Preserving Energy

1. **Prioritize Rest**: Ensure adequate rest and sleep to conserve energy. Construct a comfortable shelter and allocate time for essential activities, such as gathering food, without overexerting yourself.

2. **Efficient Movement**: Optimize movement by choosing the easiest paths through the terrain. Minimize unnecessary climbs or descents, and conserve energy by moving steadily instead of rushing.

3. **Strategic Meal Timing**: Plan meals strategically, consuming energy-rich foods when needed most. Eating smaller, frequent

meals can help maintain a steady energy level.

4. **Hydration**: Stay well-hydrated to support bodily functions and prevent fatigue. Dehydration can significantly impact energy levels, making it essential to drink water regularly.

**Example Scenario:** Recognizing the need for energy conservation, you prioritize rest during the hottest part of the day, utilizing the shelter you've constructed. When moving through the wilderness, you choose paths that require less effort, preserving your energy for essential activities.

By following these detailed instructions and examples for obtaining food through edible plants, basic foraging tips, fishing and trapping, and energy preservation, lost hikers can sustain themselves in the wilderness, ensuring vital nutrition and energy for the challenges that lie ahead. These techniques, rooted in resourcefulness and adaptability, are crucial for surviving in a challenging and unpredictable environment.

8

# Signaling for Rescue

**C**hapter 8:

In a survival situation, effective signaling can be the difference between being located quickly and prolonged isolation. This chapter provides detailed instructions, methods, techniques, and examples for signaling for rescue through building a signal fire, using signaling devices such as whistles, signal mirrors, and flashlights, as well as creating visible markers.

**A. Building a Signal Fire**

1. **Selecting a Location**: Choose an open area with a clear line of sight to the sky. Ensure the chosen spot is free of overhanging branches and other flammable materials that may pose a fire hazard.

2. **Gather Dry Fuel**: Collect a sufficient amount of dry, combustible materials like leaves, twigs, and bark. Ensure the materials are as dry as possible to facilitate quick ignition.

3. **Building a Pyramid Fire**: Arrange the collected fuel in a pyramid shape. This configuration allows the fire to burn steadily and produce a significant amount of smoke.

4. **Using Greenery for Smoke**: Add green, non-poisonous vegetation to the fire to create more smoke. This enhances the fire's visibility, making it an effective daytime signaling method.

5. **Maintaining the Fire**: Keep the fire well-fed with dry fuel to sustain a continuous column of smoke. Periodically adjust the size and shape of the pyramid to maintain a steady signal.

**Example Scenario:** As you spot an aircraft in the distance, you quickly gather dry leaves, twigs, and some green branches. Building a well-structured pyramid fire, you ignite it, generating a thick column of smoke that catches the attention of the passing plane.

**B. Use of Signaling Devices**

1. **Whistles**
2. a. **Selecting a High-Pitched Whistle**: Choose a whistle with a high-pitched sound that can travel long distances. The piercing sound is more likely to cut through ambient noise.
3. b. **Establishing Signal Patterns**: Use a distinct pattern for signaling, such as three short blasts followed by a pause. This pattern is widely recognized as a distress signal.
4. c. **Timing and Repetition**: Space out whistle signals with regular intervals to prevent confusion. Repeat the pattern consistently to increase the chances of being heard.
5. **Signal Mirrors**
6. a. **Aiming the Mirror**: Hold the signal mirror with both hands, aligning it to reflect sunlight towards the intended target. Aim the reflected light in the direction of potential rescuers.
7. b. **Flashing Morse Code**: If within sight distance, use Morse Code to send simple messages by tilting the mirror to create flashes. The international distress signal "SOS" (...—-...) is universally recognized.

8. c. **Using the Mirror at Night**: Signal mirrors with built-in aiming devices can also be effective at night when reflecting moonlight towards potential rescuers.

9. **Flashlights**

10. a. **Selecting a Powerful Flashlight**: Choose a flashlight with a powerful beam and a long-range. LED flashlights are often more efficient for signaling.

11. b. **Creating Distinct Signals**: Use flashlight signals at night by turning the light on and off in a distinct pattern. Similar to whistles, create recognizable sequences like three short flashes followed by a pause.

12. c. **Utilizing Morse Code**: Signal messages using Morse Code by turning the flashlight on and off. The international distress signal "SOS" can be conveyed with three short flashes, three long flashes, and three short flashes (...—-...).

## C. Creating Visible Markers

1. **Clothing and Gear**: Use brightly colored clothing or gear to create visible markers. Tie these items to trees, branches, or other elevated locations to increase visibility.

2. **Ground Markers**: Create ground markers using rocks, sticks, or other contrasting materials arranged in recognizable patterns or symbols. This can be especially effective in open areas.

3. **Signal Panels**: If available, use signal panels or improvised materials (such as a space blanket) to create large, reflective surfaces visible from the air.

**Example Scenario:** In the dense forest, you hear the distant sound of a helicopter. Grabbing your high-pitched whistle, you blow three short bursts followed by a pause. Simultaneously, you use your signal mirror to reflect sunlight towards the approaching helicopter, creating a combination of audible and visual signals.

By mastering the techniques outlined for building a signal fire, using signaling devices like whistles, signal mirrors, and flashlights, as well as creating visible markers, lost hikers significantly increase their chances of being rescued. These methods leverage both sight and sound to communicate distress signals effectively, ensuring that rescue teams can locate individuals in need of assistance.

9

# Communication with Search and Rescue

**C**hapter 9:

In a survival scenario, effective communication with search and rescue (**SAR**) teams is paramount. This chapter provides detailed instructions, methods, techniques, and examples for communicating with **SAR** through the use of emergency communication devices, sounding distress signals, and creating visible signals.

## A. Use of Emergency Communication Devices

1. **Personal Locator Beacon (PLB)**
2. a. **Activation**: In case of an emergency, activate your **PLB**. Ensure it is in an open area with a clear view of the sky to allow satellite communication.
3. b. **Wait for Signal Acquisition**: Be patient and wait for the **PLB** to acquire a GPS fix and transmit your distress signal to **SAR**. This process may take some time, so refrain from moving around excessively.
4. c. **Avoid Obstructions**: Keep the **PLB** away from large obstructions like cliffs or dense tree cover that may hinder the signal's

transmission.

5. **Satellite Messengers**

6. a. **Message Composition**: Compose concise and clear messages when using satellite messengers.  Include relevant information such as your location, the nature of the emergency, and the number of individuals in your party.

7. b. **Regular Check-Ins**: Establish a schedule for regular check-ins with your emergency contacts. This helps **SAR** teams track your progress and respond swiftly in case of an emergency.

8. c. **Battery Management**: Conserve battery life by turning off the device when not in use. Carry extra batteries or a portable solar charger for extended trips.

9. **Cell Phones**

10. a. **Preserve Battery**: Preserve your cell phone's battery by using it only for essential communication. Switch to airplane mode or turn it off when not in use to conserve power.

11. b. **Send Text Messages**: In areas with weak signals, text messages may have a better chance of getting through than calls. Use text messages to convey important information concisely.

12. c. **Call 911**: If within range, dial emergency services directly. Provide your location, the nature of the emergency, and any pertinent details requested by the dispatcher.

**Example Scenario:** You activate your **PLB** after realizing you're lost in a remote area. Finding an open space, you wait patiently as the **PLB** acquires a signal. Once the distress signal is transmitted, **SAR** teams receive your location and initiate the rescue process.

**B. Sounding Distress Signals**

1. **Whistles**

2. a. **Distinct Signal Patterns**: Utilize distinct patterns when

sounding distress signals with a whistle.  Three short blasts followed by a pause is a recognized distress signal.

3. b. **Consistency is Key**: Maintain a consistent pattern to prevent confusion. If possible, establish a routine for sounding signals at regular intervals.

4. c. **Optimal Conditions**: Whistles are effective in areas with limited visibility, such as dense forests or during inclement weather. The high-pitched sound carries well over distance.

5. **Shouting and Yelling**

6. a. **Conserving Energy**: Shout only when necessary to conserve energy. Yelling loudly for extended periods can lead to exhaustion and dehydration.

7. b. **Structured Calls**: When shouting, use structured calls such as "Help!" or "Over here!" to convey your distress clearly. Pause between calls to listen for potential responses.

8. c. **Terrain Considerations**: Be mindful of your surroundings. In open areas, your shouts may carry further, while in dense forests, sound may be muffled.

9. **Firearms or Loud Devices**

10. a. **Using Gunshots**: If carrying a firearm, use it judiciously to fire three shots in rapid succession. This is a widely recognized distress signal.

11. b. **Alternative Loud Devices**: In the absence of a firearm, use other loud devices such as an air horn or an emergency whistle to create attention-grabbing noise.

12. c. **Understanding Gun Safety**: Ensure safe firearm practices and be aware of your surroundings before discharging a firearm for signaling purposes.

**Example Scenario:** You find yourself on a barren mountainside and spot a potential rescue team in the distance. Utilizing your emergency whistle, you blow three short blasts followed by a pause. The sound carries through the mountain air, alerting the rescue team to your location.

**C. Creating Visible Signals**

1. **Signal Fires**
2. a. **Colorful Smoke**: Add colored materials to your signal fire to create colorful smoke. Green vegetation, rubber, or other materials can produce distinctive colors visible from a distance.
3. b. **Reflective Surfaces**: Position reflective surfaces near the fire, such as mirrors or metal, to catch and reflect sunlight. This enhances visibility during daytime rescues.
4. c. **Size Matters**: Build a larger-than-normal fire to increase its visibility. A big, well-fed fire generates more heat and smoke, making it noticeable from afar.
5. **Brightly Colored Clothing or Gear**
6. a. **Wearable Signals**: Wear or display brightly colored clothing or gear that contrasts with the environment. This serves as a visible signal to both ground and aerial search teams.
7. b. **Conspicuous Placement**: If stationary, position yourself in an open area, making your presence more conspicuous. Stand out against the natural surroundings to attract attention.
8. c. **Creating Patterns**: Arrange clothing or gear in specific patterns or symbols to convey messages or indicate distress. This method is particularly effective in snow-covered landscapes.
9. **Signal Panels**
10. a. **Improvised Panels**: Create improvised signal panels using available materials. A space blanket, tarp, or large piece of fabric can serve as a reflective surface during daytime rescues.
11. b. **Symbolic Patterns**: Draw or arrange symbols on the signal panel that signify distress or aid. A large "X" or "SOS" can be

universally understood distress signals.

**Example Scenario:** As night falls, you decide to create a signal fire. Adding green vegetation to the fire creates colorful smoke, enhancing visibility. Nearby, you position a reflective space blanket to catch the light from the fire, creating a dual visual signal for both day and night rescues.

By implementing the methods outlined for communication with search and rescue through emergency communication devices, sounding distress signals, and creating visible signals, lost hikers significantly increase their chances of being located and rescued. These techniques leverage a combination of technology, sound, and visual cues to ensure effective communication with rescue teams, ultimately leading to a successful and timely rescue operation.

# 10

# Night Survival

**C**hapter 10:
Surviving the night in the wilderness requires careful planning and resourcefulness. This chapter provides detailed instructions, methods, techniques, and examples for prioritizing warmth, establishing safe sleeping arrangements, and monitoring your surroundings during the night.

## A. Prioritize Warmth

1. **Layering Clothing**: Dress in layers to retain body heat. Start with a moisture-wicking base layer, add an insulating layer, and finish with a waterproof outer layer to protect against the elements.
2. **Insulating Materials**: Utilize insulating materials such as fleece, down, or synthetic fabrics. These materials trap warm air close to the body, providing essential insulation in cold conditions.
3. **Emergency Blankets**: Carry emergency or space blankets to reflect and retain body heat. Wrap yourself in the blanket, ensuring it covers your entire body to maximize its effectiveness.
4. **Firecraft Skills**: If possible, build a small, controlled fire. The heat generated not only provides warmth but also boosts morale.

Use dry and easily combustible materials to start and maintain the fire.

**Example Scenario:** As temperatures drop during the night, you layer your clothing, wearing a moisture-wicking base layer, an insulating fleece jacket, and a waterproof shell. Additionally, you unfold your emergency blanket, wrapping it around yourself while sitting by a carefully managed campfire.

**B. Safe Sleeping Arrangements**

1. **Insulated Sleeping Surface**: Create an insulated barrier between your body and the cold ground. Use materials like pine needles, leaves, or a sleeping pad to minimize heat loss.
2. **Proper Sleeping Bag Usage**: Enter your sleeping bag fully clothed, with extra layers if needed. Cinch the hood around your head to retain warmth. Avoid breathing inside the bag to prevent moisture buildup.
3. **Shelter Considerations**: If using a tent or improvised shelter, ensure it is well-ventilated to prevent condensation. Condensation inside the shelter can make clothing and bedding damp, reducing their insulating properties.
4. **Body Heat Conservation**: If sharing a sleeping space with others, huddle together to conserve body heat. The collective warmth generated by a group can significantly improve overall comfort.

**Example Scenario:** In your improvised shelter, you spread a thick layer of pine needles on the ground for insulation. Inside your sleeping bag, you wear an additional layer of clothing, cinching the hood tightly. Sharing the shelter with a fellow hiker, you both benefit from the combined body heat.

**C. Monitoring Surroundings**

1. **Night Vision Preservation**: Allow your eyes to adjust to the darkness. Minimize the use of artificial light sources to preserve night vision, which is crucial for navigating and monitoring your surroundings.

2. **Listening for Wildlife**: Pay attention to sounds in the environment. Familiarize yourself with normal nocturnal wildlife sounds to distinguish them from potential threats.

3. **Observing Sky Conditions**: If the sky is clear, take advantage of celestial navigation. Familiarize yourself with prominent constellations and use them to determine direction.

4. **Regular Check-Ins**: Periodically wake up during the night to assess your surroundings. Check for changes in weather conditions, potential dangers, or signs of nearby wildlife.

**Example Scenario:** As night falls, you refrain from using your flashlight to preserve night vision. You listen for the rustle of nocturnal creatures and identify the distant calls of owls. During a brief wake-up, you notice a shift in wind direction, prompting you to adjust the positioning of your shelter for added protection.

Surviving the night in the wilderness requires a combination of proactive measures, preparedness, and adaptability. By prioritizing warmth through proper clothing and firecraft skills, establishing safe sleeping arrangements, and consistently monitoring your surroundings, you enhance your chances of a comfortable and secure night survival experience. These techniques are essential for maintaining well-being and readiness in the unpredictable environment of the wilderness after dark.

# 11

# Psychological Resilience

**C**hapter 11:
Surviving in the wilderness isn't just about physical prowess; psychological resilience plays a crucial role in navigating the challenges of the unknown. This chapter provides detailed instructions, methods, techniques, and examples for maintaining a positive mindset, coping with fear and anxiety, and engaging in activities to stay occupied.

A. **Maintaining a Positive Mindset**

1. **Mindfulness Practices**: Incorporate mindfulness techniques to stay present and focused. Engage in deep breathing exercises, meditation, or simply observe your surroundings to anchor yourself in the present moment.
2. **Positive Self-Talk**: Counter negative thoughts with positive affirmations. Remind yourself of your capabilities, past successes, and the resilience you've demonstrated in overcoming challenges.
3. **Goal Setting**: Establish realistic and achievable short-term goals. Celebrate small victories, such as successfully starting a fire or navigating through challenging terrain, to boost morale.

4. **Gratitude Reflection**: Reflect on positive aspects of your situation. Express gratitude for the resources and skills you possess, fostering a sense of appreciation even in challenging circumstances.

**Example Scenario:** Caught in a sudden rainstorm, you find yourself feeling disheartened. Practicing mindfulness, you focus on the sound of raindrops and the sensation of water on your skin. Reminding yourself that rainwater is a valuable resource, you embrace the moment and adapt to the changing weather with a positive mindset.

B. **Coping with Fear and Anxiety**

1. **Acknowledge Emotions**: Recognize and acknowledge feelings of fear or anxiety. Suppressing emotions can intensify them, while acknowledging them allows for better emotional regulation.
2. **Fear Hierarchy**: If specific fears arise, create a fear hierarchy. Break down fears into manageable steps and gradually expose yourself to them, allowing for a gradual desensitization process.
3. **Visualization Techniques**: Use visualization to imagine successful outcomes. Picture yourself overcoming challenges, finding your way back, or successfully signaling for rescue. Visualization can help alleviate anxiety and instill confidence.
4. **Grounding Techniques**: Practice grounding techniques to stay rooted in the present. Focus on physical sensations, such as the texture of the ground beneath you or the feeling of the wind on your face, to reduce anxiety.

**Example Scenario:** As night falls, fear of the unknown starts to creep in. Acknowledging this, you create a fear hierarchy, breaking down concerns about wildlife encounters into manageable steps. Through visualization, you imagine successfully navigating the night, calming your anxiety and gaining a sense of control.

## C. Engaging in Activities to Stay Occupied

1. **Resourceful Hobbies**: Engage in resourceful and purposeful activities. Collect firewood, forage for edible plants, or organize your survival gear. Keeping occupied with essential tasks helps maintain focus and a sense of purpose.
2. **Journaling**: Document your experiences, thoughts, and observations in a journal. Journaling provides a creative outlet, helps process emotions, and serves as a valuable record of your journey.
3. **Observational Skills**: Sharpen your observational skills by studying the natural environment. Identify animal tracks, bird calls, or unique plant species. This not only keeps you occupied but enhances your connection with the wilderness.
4. **Mental Games**: Play mental games to stay sharp. Challenge yourself with memory exercises, mental math, or riddles. Keeping the mind active can distract from negative thoughts and anxiety.

**Example Scenario:** Facing an extended period of waiting, you decide to organize your survival gear. As you meticulously arrange items and take inventory, you engage in purposeful activity, keeping your mind occupied. Later, you document your experiences in your journal, reflecting on the challenges faced and lessons learned.

Psychological resilience is a vital component of wilderness survival. By maintaining a positive mindset, coping with fear and anxiety through acknowledgment and visualization, and engaging in purposeful activities, you enhance your ability to adapt and thrive in challenging situations. These techniques not only contribute to your mental well-being but also serve as invaluable tools for navigating the psychological aspects of the wilderness.

<h1 style="text-align:center">12</h1>

# additional tips and considerations

**C**hapter 12:
As you navigate the wilderness, certain tips and consider-ations can further enhance your survival skills. This chapter provides detailed instructions, methods, techniques, and examples for utilizing natural resources, handling wildlife encounters, administering basic first aid in the wilderness, and navigating different terrains.

**A. Utilizing Natural Resources**

1. **Edible Plants Identification**: Expand your knowledge of edible plants specific to the region. Learn to identify safe and nutritious plant species, allowing you to supplement your diet with natural resources.

2. **Purifying Water Naturally**: In addition to traditional purifica-tion methods, explore natural water purification techniques. Solar stills, evaporation traps, and using vegetation to filter water are methods to consider in resourceful water procurement.

3. **Natural Cordage and Tools**: Craft cordage from plant fibers, such as nettles or yucca, for binding and securing items. Utilize rocks for tool creation, such as shaping arrowheads or creating

cutting edges for survival tasks.

4. **Fire Ignition from Natural Sources**: Master the art of fire ignition using natural sources. Practice friction fire methods like bow-drill or hand-drill techniques, and identify suitable tinder materials such as dry grass or bark.

**Example Scenario:** In a dense forest, you identify a stand of cattails near a water source. Recognizing them as a versatile edible plant, you harvest young shoots and roots. Nearby, you find suitable rocks for crafting primitive tools, showcasing the resourcefulness of utilizing natural elements.

**B. Wildlife Encounters**

1. **Avoiding Confrontations**: Be aware of wildlife habitats and potential encounters. Make noise to alert animals of your presence, reducing the likelihood of surprising them. Avoid getting between a mother and her young, and give wild animals plenty of space.

2. **Understanding Animal Behavior**: Familiarize yourself with the behavior of local wildlife. Recognize signs of agitation or distress in animals, and respond accordingly by calmly backing away to avoid provocation.

3. **Food Storage Practices**: Securely store food to prevent wildlife attraction to your campsite. Hang food in bear-resistant bags or use bear canisters. Avoid storing food in your sleeping area to deter nocturnal visitors.

4. **Emergency Response to Animal Attacks**: In the rare event of an animal attack, understand proper responses. Play dead for grizzly bears, fight back against black bears, and use deterrents like bear spray. For other wildlife, create distance without turning your back.

**Example Scenario:** While hiking, you encounter a black bear foraging for berries. To avoid surprising the bear, you speak calmly and back away slowly. The bear, aware of your presence, continues its activities, highlighting the importance of understanding animal behavior in preventing confrontations.

### C. Basic First Aid in the Wilderness

1. **Wound Care and Dressings**: Clean wounds promptly with sanitized water and dress them with sterile bandages. Familiarize yourself with basic wound-closure techniques, such as butterfly bandages, to minimize infection risks.
2. **Wilderness-Specific Ailments**: Be prepared for common wilderness ailments. Carry medications for allergies, pain relief, and diarrhea. Know how to identify and treat issues like poison ivy or insect bites.
3. **Improvised Splints and Braces**: In the absence of medical supplies, learn to improvise splints and braces from available materials. Stabilize fractures and sprains to prevent further injury during evacuation.
4. **Signal for Medical Assistance**: Use signaling techniques previously discussed to attract attention in medical emergencies. Create visible signals and use emergency communication devices to alert search and rescue teams.

**Example Scenario:** While traversing rocky terrain, a fellow hiker suffers a sprained ankle. You quickly assess the situation, immobilize the injured ankle using a makeshift splint, and signal for medical assistance using a combination of a brightly colored signal panel and a whistle.

### D. How to Navigate Different Terrains

1. **Wooded Areas Navigation**: In dense forests, use natural land-

marks like distinctive trees or rock formations for navigation. Maintain a sense of direction through periodic map and compass checks, ensuring you stay on course.

2. **Mountainous Terrain Navigation**: When navigating mountainous terrain, follow ridgelines or contour lines to maintain elevation. Use topographical maps to identify prominent peaks and valleys, and be mindful of changes in altitude.

3. **Desert Navigation**: In arid environments, rely on distinct features like rock formations, sand dunes, or mountain ranges for orientation. Be vigilant in tracking your water consumption and use the sun's position for direction.

4. **Coastal Navigation**: Along coastlines, utilize landmarks like cliffs, distinctive rock formations, or lighthouses. Pay attention to tidal movements and use them as additional navigational cues.

**Example Scenario:** Navigating through a dense forest, you use a combination of map and compass readings to follow a designated route. Periodically checking your surroundings against the map, you identify a unique rock formation, confirming your position and successful navigation.

By incorporating these additional tips and considerations into your wilderness survival toolkit, you enhance your ability to adapt and thrive in diverse environments. From utilizing natural resources to handling wildlife encounters, administering basic first aid, and navigating various terrains, these techniques contribute to a comprehensive skill set for overcoming the challenges of the wilderness.

# 13

## conclusion

**C**hapter XIII: Conclusion
As we conclude this guide, it's crucial to recap key survival strategies that can make the difference between adversity and triumph in the wilderness. Additionally, a source of encouragement and hope will provide the mental fortitude needed to navigate the challenges that may lie ahead.

### A. Recap of Key Survival Strategies

1. **Preparation Is Paramount**: The importance of thorough pre-trip preparations cannot be overstated. Share your itinerary, pack essential items, and equip yourself with the knowledge of navigation, shelter-building, and basic survival skills.

2. **Stay Calm and Assess the Situation**: If lost, remember to stop and stay put. Evaluate your surroundings, take stock of available resources, and mentally prepare yourself for the challenges ahead. Panic is your adversary; composure is your ally.

3. **Navigation Techniques**: Master the art of map reading, use a compass effectively, identify landmarks, and utilize celestial bodies for direction. A keen understanding of navigation techniques

ensures that you remain on the right course even in unfamiliar territory.

4. **Building Shelter**: Whether it's choosing a safe location, crafting an emergency shelter from available materials, or using clothing for insulation, shelter-building is a fundamental skill. It provides protection from the elements and is integral to surviving the night.

5. **Securing Water**: Locate water sources, understand purification methods, and remember the importance of hydration. Water is a life-sustaining resource, and knowing how to obtain and purify it is essential for survival.

6. **Obtaining Food**: Familiarize yourself with edible plants, basic foraging tips, and simple fishing and trapping techniques. Preserving energy through adequate nutrition is key to sustaining yourself during challenging times.

7. **Signaling for Rescue**: Master the art of building a signal fire, effectively use signaling devices such as whistles, signal mirrors, and flashlights, and create visible markers. Signaling increases your chances of being located and rescued.

8. **Communication with Search and Rescue**: Utilize emergency communication devices, sound distress signals, and create visible signals to communicate with search and rescue teams effectively. Clear communication is your lifeline in critical situations.

9. **Night Survival**: Prioritize warmth by layering clothing, establish safe sleeping arrangements, and consistently monitor your surroundings during the night. A comfortable and secure night's sleep is crucial for maintaining physical and mental well-being.

10. **Psychological Resilience**: Maintain a positive mindset, cope with fear and anxiety through acknowledgment and visualization, and engage in purposeful activities to stay occupied. Psychological resilience is the glue that holds your survival strategy together.

11. **Additional Tips and Considerations**: From utilizing natural

resources and handling wildlife encounters to administering basic first aid and navigating different terrains, these additional tips and considerations contribute to a comprehensive skill set for wilderness survival.

## B. Encouragement and Hope

Surviving in the wilderness demands not just physical prowess, but a resilient spirit. Throughout your journey, remember that each challenge is an opportunity to showcase your adaptability and strength. Embrace the unknown with the confidence that your acquired skills and the indomitable human spirit will see you through.

In moments of difficulty, recall the stories of those who have triumphed against the odds. Your journey is a testament to the enduring human capability to overcome, adapt, and conquer even the most formidable challenges. Encourage yourself with the knowledge that every step, every decision, brings you closer to your destination.

As you embark on your wilderness adventures, may this guide serve as a reliable companion, equipping you with the tools needed for survival and empowering you with the resilience necessary for success. The wilderness, with its challenges and mysteries, awaits your exploration, and you, armed with knowledge and fortitude, are ready to conquer it. Safe travels, adventurer, and may the wilderness unveil its wonders in the most unexpected of ways.